Coloring
THE
Psalms

A coloring book of 20 most-loved Bible verses
with floral backgrounds for girls and women

KINGDOM
CONTENTS
JOURNALS, BOOKS & MORE

This coloring book
belongs to:

_____

Date

_____

Hey!

We are happy that you have this book in your hands and we hope you will enjoy coloring in its pages!

We wanted to create something that could boost your creativity and at the same time help you to learn and memorize some of the most important words ever written in history! God's word itself!

Our prayer is that these truths can become precious to your heart and an essential part of your life.

May God bless you!

The Kingdom Contents team

I will give thanks to you, LORD, with all my heart; I will tell of all your wonderful deeds.

Psalm 9:1

The law of the Lord is perfect, refreshing the soul. The statutes of the Lord are trustworthy, making wise the simple.

Psalm 19:7

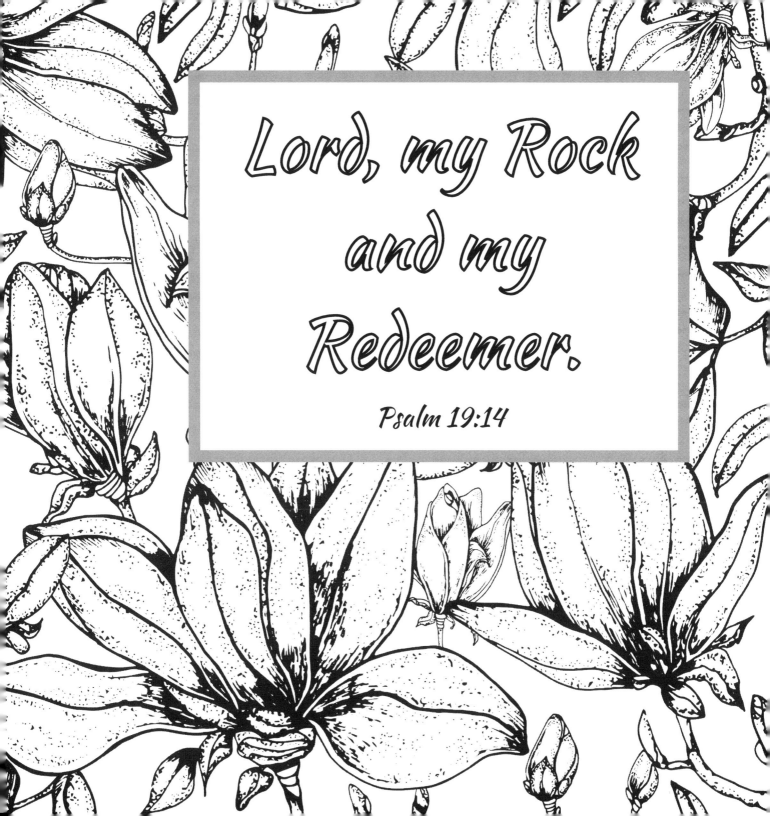

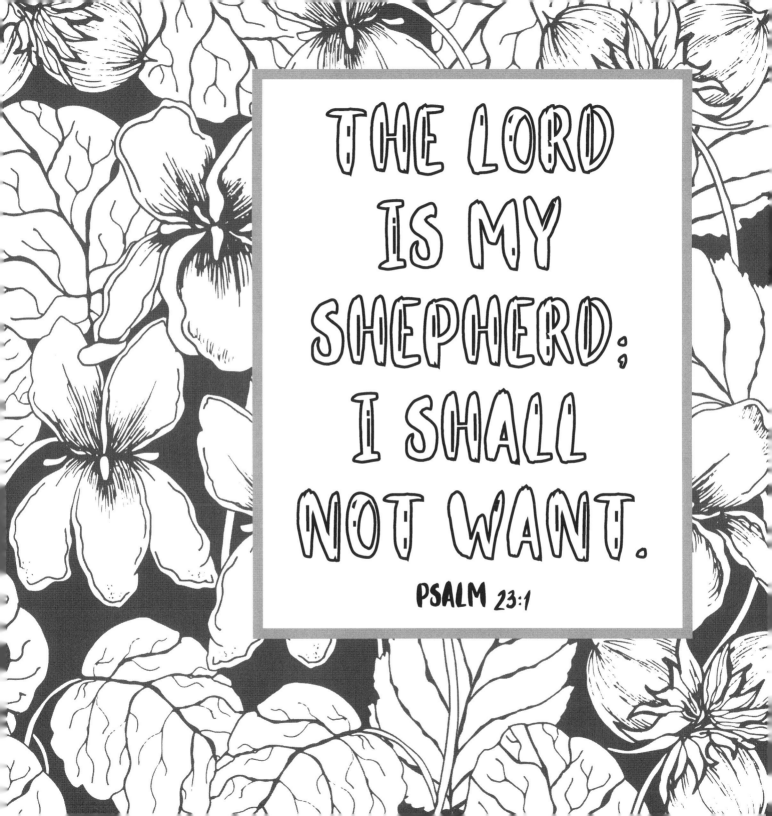

Lord my God, I called to you for help, and you healed me.

Psalm 30:2

The righteous person may have many troubles, but the Lord delivers him from them all.

Psalm 34:19

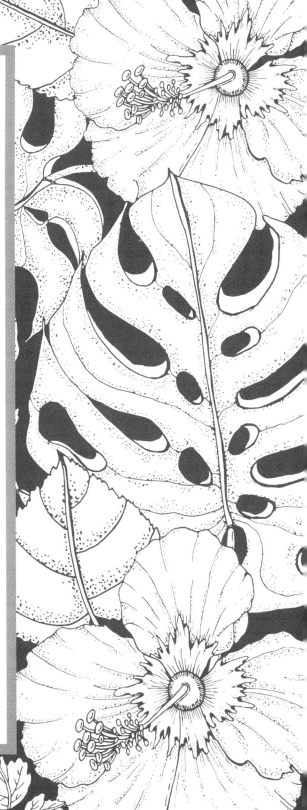

GOD IS OUR REFUGE AND STRENGTH, AN EVER-PRESENT HELP IN TROUBLE.

PSALM 46:1

Cast your cares on the Lord and he will sustain you; he will never let the righteous be shaken.

Psalm 55:22

For great is your love, reaching to the heavens; your faithfulness reaches to the skies.

Psalm 57:10

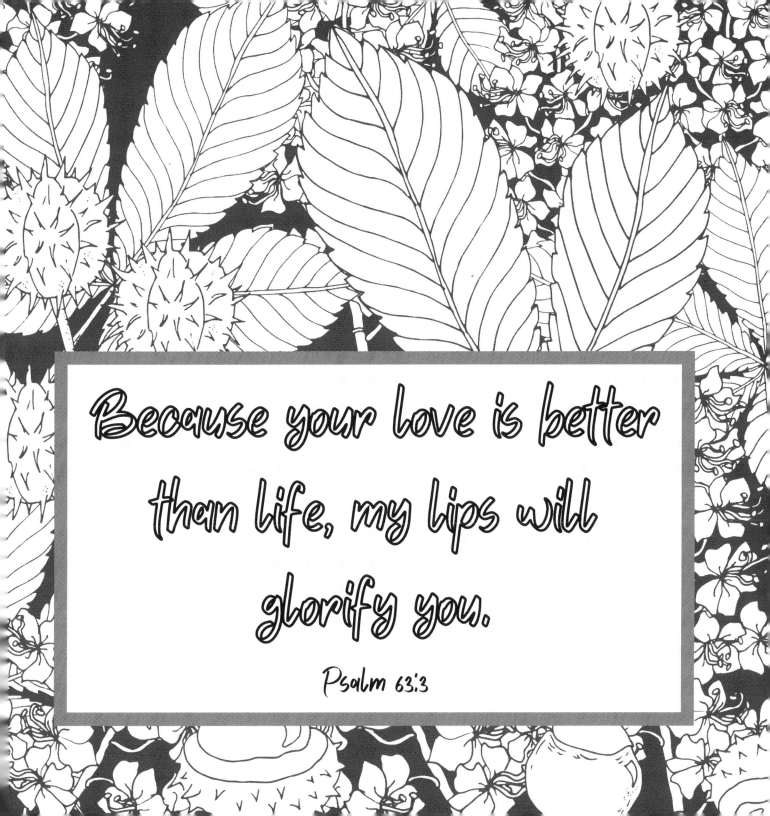

Because your love is better than life, my lips will glorify you.

Psalm 63:3

When we were overwhelmed by sins, you forgave our transgressions.

Psalm 65:3

Praise be to God, who has not rejected my prayer or withheld his love from me!

PSALM 66:20

My flesh and my heart may fail, but God is the strength of my heart and my portion forever.

Psalm 73:26

I WILL SING OF THE LORD'S GREAT LOVE FOREVER.

PSALM 89:1A

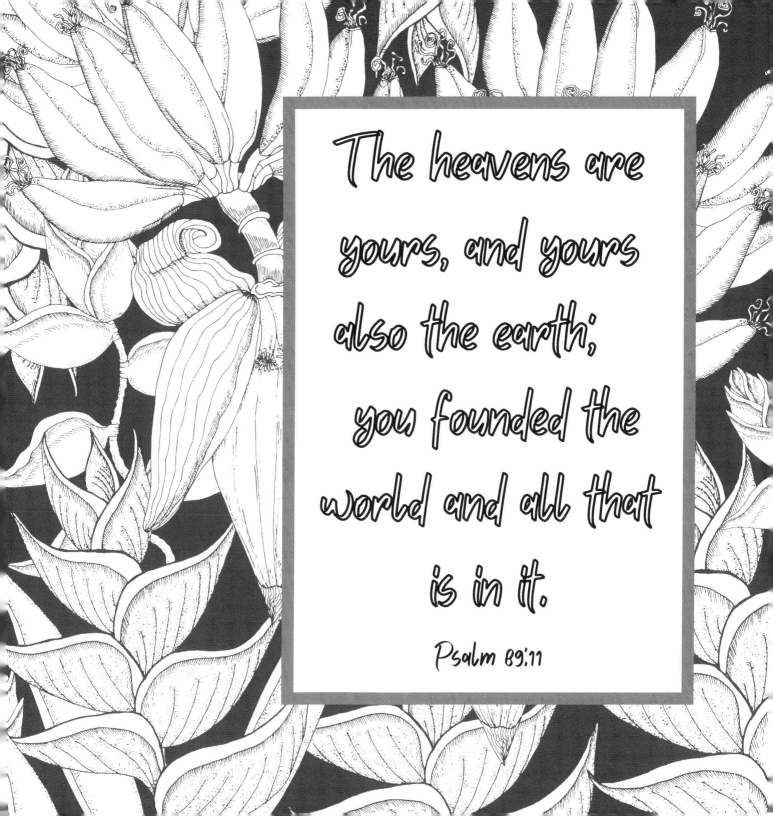

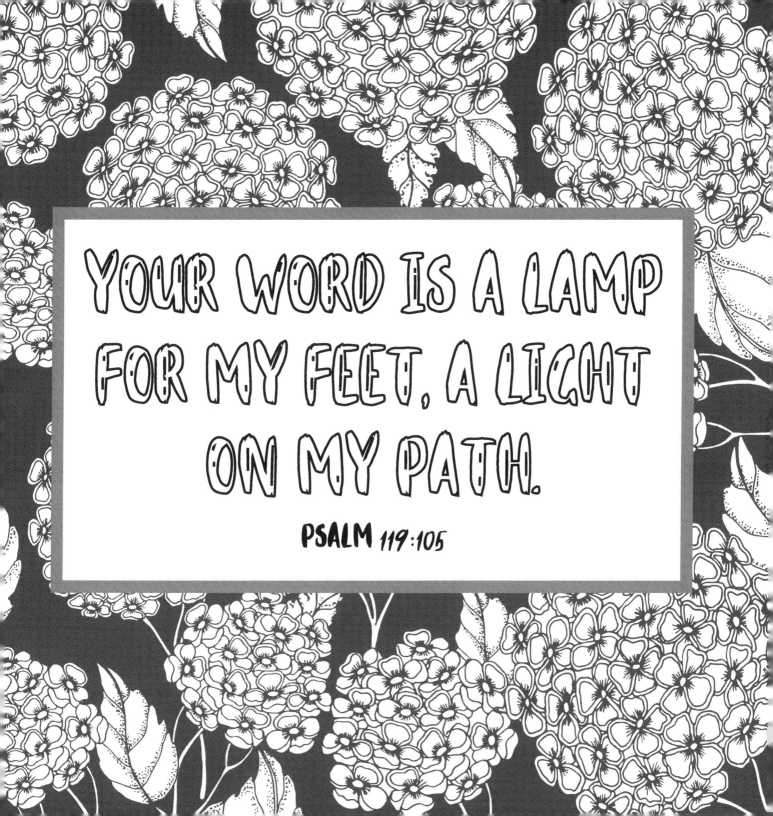

KINGDOM
CONTENTS

JOURNALS, BOOKS & MORE

We would love to hear from you!

We are always working to improve our products and create new ones. Feel
free to share any ideas and comments with us -
we appreciate your feedback and reviews!

Also, let's keep in touch through social media!

kingdomcontents

@kingdomcontents

Made in United States
Troutdale, OR
10/20/2023